HOW TO CLEAN OUT YOUR PARENTS' ESTATE IN 30 DAYS OR LESS

A Solutions-Based Guide to Emptying the Home Without Losing Your Mind

By Julie Hall
The Estate Lady®

The Estate Lady Publications
6420-A1 Rea Road #135, Charlotte NC 28277
www.theestatelady.com
704.543.1051

Credits:
Domna V. Colepaugh, Assistant

Second Edition, March 2011

Library of Congress Control Number: 2010923711

ISBN: 978-0-9844191-4-2

Printed in the United States of America.

For rights or permissions inquiries, please contact
The Estate Lady® at Julie@TheEstateLady.com

For information about custom editions, special sales, premium or corporate packages,
please contact The Estate Lady® at 704.543.1051 or at Julie@TheEstateLady.com

For all my clients–
past, present and future.

Thank you for sharing your lives so I could
learn how to serve you in a greater capacity.

Table of Contents

About the Author

Julie Hall, author of *The Boomer Burden, Dealing With Your Parent's Lifetime Accumulation of Stuff*, is an accredited personal property appraiser, estate sales professional, residential content removal specialist, and a broker of fine items. As owner and operator of The Estate Lady®, LLC, which offers turnkey estate dissolution services, she brings eighteen years of experience to families facing the overwhelming task of sorting through and emptying their parents' home. Her expertise is called upon for consulting, conducting on-site estate sales, appraising personal property, and organizing the removal and disposal of contents in the most appropriate way.

In addition to her responsibilities as The Estate Lady®, Julie's passion for helping as many distressed families as possible deal with the challenges of estate dissolution inspired her to take ownership of the American Society of Estate Liquidators ® (ASEL) in 2007. As director of ASEL, her vision is to dedicate the organization to being an educational and referral resource to estate liquidation professionals nationwide. Today, ASEL offers educational courses, resources, products, and support to industry professionals and those interested in becoming estate liquidators.

A popular speaker to groups dealing with older adult issues and estate accumulation challenges, she is also an expert author on many senior and boomer websites, answering questions about appraisals, downsizing, and family matters. Her work has been published in The Wall Street Journal, Bloomberg News, MSN Money, LA Times, etc, and she is called upon by people worldwide for her sound advice.

In 2007, The Estate Lady®, LLC was selected by StartupNation as one of the top three home-based businesses in the United States in its Boomers Back in Business category.

Julie is an accredited member of Association of Online Appraisers, the Certified Appraisers Guild of America, the National Speakers Association, the National Association of Women Business Owners, and the Better Business Bureau. Julie resides in Charlotte, North Carolina, with her family.

For more information, please visit Julie's websites: www.TheEstateLady.com, www.ASELonline.com, www.TheBoomerBurden.com or her blog at http://estatelady.wordpress.com

Introduction

With all my years in the estate industry, the one thing I keep hearing over and over is how my boomer clients wish they had a simple, step-by-step, "how to" guide to point them in the right direction after beloved parents become infirm and/or pass away. I have dedicated my career to being a resource for clients and empowering them with knowledge to take on this overwhelming responsibility.

I want you to be prepared for what's coming. There is much to do both before and after parents leave us. Knowing the correct order in which to do the numerous necessary tasks will make your life much less overwhelming. I hope this guide will act as a friendly hand to hold during the process.

This guide is complimentary to my book, *The Boomer Burden – Dealing With Your Parents' Lifetime Accumulation of Stuff,* available on Amazon and at all major booksellers. Having hit #1 in several different categories, its reviews are tremendous. People email me from all over the world thanking me for writing it. With 100+ million of us needing this guidance, I would recommend picking up the book if you have not yet done so. If you have already read it, this guide is an additional resource and will act as a working manual to put in your purse or briefcase to check things off as you go.

My goal is to make this overwhelming process as easy as possible for you, all the while making you aware of things most people never even think about. You need a quick-reference, easy to understand, easy to follow guide that provides you with peace of mind and keeps it "simple."

This is a topic that is touching 78 million Baby Boomers and 45 million of their parents. Timely and relevant for today's aging population, this daunting issue is rarely talked about until now. I know this guide will offer you trustworthy guidance and lighten *your* load during this very difficult time in your life.

Section I

One or Both Parents Are Living & Still in Their Home

HAVING THAT HEART TO HEART: PLANNING FOR THE INEVITABLE

If one or both of your parents are still living and mentally competent, preparing for the transition also means preparing for the inevitable. You need to begin talking to your parents about the future. Topics you need to cover include:

☐ Monthly bills and expenses

☐ Medications list and other related health information: Medical records, List of doctors with contact info, signed HIPPA forms

☐ Location of important papers including:

Wills/Trusts	Bank accounts	Investment accounts
Insurance policies	Mortgages	Outstanding Loans
Pensions	Deeds and titles	Retirement accounts
Safety deposit boxes	Credit Accounts	Stashed valuables
Computer passwords		

(A complete checklist and tracking document for important papers is in Section VI of this manual)

☐ The existence of a will and whether it is up-to-date according to his/her/their wishes

Division of assets	Name of executor
Financial power of attorney	Healthcare power of attorney
Durable power of attorney	Special bequests

☐ Alternatives to the family home should health or limitations dictate a move

Retirement community	Assisted living center	Nursing facility
Live with family member		

☐ End-of-life decisions

Obituary wording	Burial preferences	Cremation preferences

Funeral preferences (eulogy, music, specific readings, who conducts service)
Memorial preference in lieu of flowers

☐ Living bequests – Discuss the possibility of certain sentimental items being given to children, grandchildren, and heirs, while parents are still living versus after death. This can significantly minimize feuding after the death of a loved one.

Conversation Starters

It is never easy to talk with your parents about future issues. Here are some conversation starters that will make it more comfortable for you and your parents:

"Dad, something's been on my mind I wanted to talk with you about. Maybe now is a good time to talk about a plan for when something happens to you or mom. I want to make sure I know what to do when the time comes and I need your help."

"Sue and I have some concerns after you are gone. We'd like to talk with you and make sure you have all your documents like a will/trust, power of attorney, etc. Can you tell us your plan so we don't argue?"

"Bob and I would like to know your plan and final wishes. If you don't have a plan in place, we would like to help you so we will know everything to do and it will be done as you would like."

"Mom and Dad, sometimes I worry about you living all alone. Are there any things we could do to help you?"

"Dad, when Uncle Jim passed away, his family fought for weeks over things. Do you ever worry that Mike and I will be like that?"

"Jim and I started looking closer at our retirement account, and we'd love to pick your brain about all the things we need to know about retirement."

"Dad, do you ever worry about Mom if she had to go on alone without you?"

Parents, listen to your children. And children, listen to your parents. This is a critical conversation for all of you and you want to make sure you communicate well. Just like when we were kids in school, don't be afraid to raise your hand and ask questions. Making assumptions or guessing about what the other one wants can be dangerous and lead to places you don't want to go. Remember what your teachers used to tell you. There's no such thing as a dumb question.

PROTECTING FROM FRAUD

The unfortunate reality is that the elderly are preyed upon worse than any other demographic population. Protecting your parents from fraud and scams will avoid discovering surprises and unexpected losses in the future.

To follow are six things you should do to protect your parents from fraudulent activities:

☐ Ask or discuss with your parents who has durable power of attorney.

☐ Register your parents' telephone number(s) with the National Do Not Call Registry (www.donotcall.gov).

☐ Discuss with them the list of common frauds (outlined in this chapter) and ask them to contact you if they suspect anyone is trying to defraud them.

☐ Ask your parents to contact you if anyone offers to buy any of their possessions.

☐ Make sure a family member personally visits your parents on a weekly basis. If this is a challenge and you have other siblings, take turns.

☐ Reduce junk mail for a small fee by going to either of these Web sites: www.stopthejunkmail.com and www.greendimes.com.

A complete overview of scams, schemes and fraudulent activities commonly attempted on the elderly are listed in *The Boomer Burden – Dealing With Your Parent's Lifetime Accumulation of Stuff*.

UPDATING/ORGANIZING PAPERWORK

Being organized now before any transition or the inevitable occurs will save much anguish and frustration for you and your family.

☐ Last Will and Testament/Trust is up-to-date
> Was it legally prepared, witnessed and/or notarized?
> Family changes affecting distribution are currently reflected including recent illness, deaths, births, adoptions, marriages, and divorces
> Property changes are up-to-date
> Tax law changes have been considered and addressed
> Residence changes are up-to-date
> Beneficiaries match those identified in insurance or investment papers
> Original stored in a fire-proof safe or off premises in safe deposit box
> Copy given to executor or attorney
> Location of will has been identified and is known by you and other key family members, siblings

☐ Financial assets and investments are itemized and organized
> Records and reporting statements in known location
> Account numbers and access information are in a safe, known location
> Bank account and retirement account numbers and access are safe, in known location
> Computer passwords for accounts are in a safe, known location
> Record of contents in the safe deposit box (es), possibly add additional signature on box, and know where the keys are

☐ Insurance policies are valid, current and organized

☐ Real property mortgage, deeds, and titles are itemized and organized

☐ Personal property and known valuables are itemized and documented
> Antiques   Collectibles   Fine art
> Gold/Silver   Jewelry   China/Crystal

☐ Stashed Valuables
> Be sure to ask your parents if there are any known stashes in the house or on the grounds (gold coins, jewelry, cash, stock certificates, etc). Note: Reference page 39 for the listing of places to look.

Living Revocable Trust

A living revocable trust is an alternative to a will. When deciding between a will and a living revocable trust, it is best to seek legal counsel.

To follow are a few basics about a living revocable trust:

- Does not need to be administered by probate court

- Gives instructions for distribution of property upon death

- Goes into effect if unable to handle financial or personal affairs due to incapacity or disability

- Transfers ownership of property to a designated trustee

- Identifies beneficiaries

- Identifies a successor trustee

- Can be finalized more quickly than a will

NOTES:

_____

_____

_____

_____

_____

_____

Section II

One or Both Parents
Are Living &
in Failing Health

PREPARING FOR THE TRANSITION

Part of preparing for a transition is to understand the available resources in your parents' community, or your community, should additional support be needed as your parents begin to show signs of failing health. If the transition can occur over time, then some resources can be used as a means of providing support and care while still in their home. Prepare in advance of the crisis, and maintain a folder of these resources.

☐ Consult a geriatric care manager in the area (http://www.caremanager.org).

☐ Seek out community resources offering support to senior citizens at home.

Meals on Wheels	Senior citizen centers	Churches
Synagogues	Christian Ministries	Respite Care
Adult Day Care	Companion care at home	

☐ Make frequent visits and daily phone calls a part of the routine.

☐ Alert parents' neighbors.

☐ Notify local law enforcement and emergency personnel.

☐ Install home alarm or video monitoring system.

☐ Consider adding a trusted, local family member to bank accounts to assist with bill payment.

☐ Consider ordering a medical alert device.

☐ Investigate hiring a home health care nurse (in home care, either skilled or non-skilled).

☐ Consider the demands placed upon the nearest sibling or family member.

☐ Consider home modification or equipment needed to extend parents' home stay.

Railings	Bathroom fixtures	Stair lift
Door handles	Move bed to first floor	Multiple walkers
Potty chairs	Elevated toilet seat	Grippers /arm extenders
Entrance ramp	Check door widths (3 ft)	Hallway widths (3 ft)
Roll-under sink	Light switch heights	

☐ Obtain aids for parents such as pill distribution system, magnifiers, non-skid mats.

THE RELOCATION DECISION

With the eventual likelihood that they will need to be relocated, part of what needs to be decided is if they would relocate to live with or near you, another sibling, or stay in their hometown. To make the best decision for all, use these guidelines:

☐ Talk about it – What do your parents want? What are their wishes?

☐ Don't wait until a crisis – many places have 1-3 year long waiting lists

☐ When discussing a new residence or lifestyle change, consider bringing in a Geriatric Care Manager (www.NAPGCM.com). They will assess needs, offer solutions and anticipate future needs.

☐ Consider their current health care level. As healthcare needs increase, new decisions will have to be made – that will be time to re-evaluate.

☐ What is the current financial situation?

☐ Can they afford assisted living? In-home health care? Go live with family member?

NOTES:

_____

_____

_____

_____

_____

_____

_____

_____

_____

_____

_____

_____

EASING THE TRANSITION

The most difficult part for your loved one is *letting go*. Suddenly, your parent(s) are being asked to let go of everything, from making everyday decisions to their much-loved home. They don't want to leave or to let go of their "things" that they worked so hard to possess. These "things" contain a lifetime of memories. You might think it is clutter, but to them, everything is precious. If mentally capable, allow parents to be a part of the decision-making.

Once it is determined that being in someone's care is essential, here are some transition guidelines and things to consider:

☐ Consider the actual square footage of the space to be occupied by your parent.

☐ Get a blueprint of the new space so furniture can be effectively placed.

☐ Determine what can realistically fit into the square footage.

☐ Determine what heirlooms need to be stored for safekeeping.

☐ Valuables should not go to a facility with them. They have a tendency to disappear while parents are either out or sleeping; often doors are left unlocked.

☐ Identify sentimental and small familiar items that can make the new space comfortable.

Pictures	Photo books	Accent items
Books	Family Bible	Favorite blanket/pillow
Hobby items	Craft supplies	Playing cards, board games

☐ Less is better. Typically too much is kept causing a tripping hazard or clutter.

☐ Be practical. Holiday decorations, books, magazines, etc do not need to go. Be minimalistic with these items as they can take up a lot of space.

☐ Be realistic. How much clothing and linens are truly needed? Loose fitting, comfortable, pull-on, or zip-up clothing items are best.

It also depends on the place in which your parent(s) are moving. Take these additional guidelines to heart depending on the scenario you are currently managing.

☐ If moving to your home or a sibling's home:
Respect that they still need to feel at home in your home.
Allow their furniture and things to be in the room they will be staying in versus just moving them into an existing guest room with its existing furnishings, etc.

☐ If moving to an assisted living center:

    You will only have one or two rooms with not much storage space.

☐ If moving to a nursing home:

    You will not need furniture and for sanitary reasons many facilities will not allow furniture into the room

NOTES:

_____

_____

_____

_____

_____

_____

_____

_____

_____

_____

_____

_____

_____

_____

_____

_____

_____

_____

_____

Leaving a Legacy

What kind of legacy will your parents leave? What stories will live on after they are gone? You, your children and grandchildren may or may not be able to recount the major events in your parents' lives. Don't wish you would have asked after your parents are gone. Start to capture these stories now. Ask them to share how these events changed their life and potentially yours as a result. Have them share how their military service, living through the Great Depression or the Civil Rights movement, growing up poor, immigrating to America, etc. impacted their thoughts and emotions. Invite them to share their stories in a way they can be preserved and remembered.

Some of the ways this can be done are:

- Writing a personal letter to each child and grandchild.

- Create a final love letter to comfort a spouse.

- Leave behind a thank you card or letter for caregiver(s).

- Ask a friend or writer to help you record written memories and stories.

- Set up a video camera to capture the memories and stories on tape.

- Have them share the stories behind special heirlooms they will inherit.

- Record them reading a favorite story.

While the thought of your parents leaving your family is painful to consider, your actions will provide great comfort and be a permanent, loving embrace to their memory and what can be passed down for generations to come.

Section III

Mom or Dad
Have Died &
the Estate Remains

TO DO IMMEDIATELY

The executor has a responsibility to protect all that the parents owned until all decisions have been made about the proper distribution and dissolution methods. The following actions are important, critical first steps to be taken by the executor or estate attorney in order to properly protect and prepare the estate on behalf of the deceased parents.

☐ Collect keys / change residential and other property locks (no exceptions, always change the locks).

☐ New master keys to be in the executor's and/or estate attorney's possession only.

☐ Notify heirs and family members that locks have been changed for security reasons.

☐ Oversee collection of all paperwork.

☐ Remove valuables (should only be done by the executor or executrix) including:
   Jewelry (gold, silver, precious, semi-precious)   Paintings or original artworks
   Sterling silver items and flatware   Bronzes, pottery
   Guns, coins, stamp or other collections   Sculptures

☐ Notify heirs and family that removal of valuables is temporary only until estate is settled.

☐ Prepare a list of all valuables to be kept in executor's or estate attorney's file for documentation.

☐ Hire a professional personal property appraiser to assess all valuables.

☐ Walk through the house and list anything of sentimental value.

☐ Walk through the house and locate anything listed as a bequest in the will.

☐ Make a copy of the created list to distribute to heirs for review.

☐ Have heirs prepare a wish list of items they would like to have/keep.

☐ Divide contents to be dispersed among heirs, with appraised values, to assure equity in distribution.

☐ Items in which several heirs want the same item:
   Determine value for the item
   Select a name from a hat, or other equitable division (one gets item, others get equivalent value in compensation)
   If the item is small, can the heirs share the item?

☐ Notify heirs and family of how estate will be managed and dispersed once determined.

☐ Gather all professionals pertinent to the estate's dissolution

Insurance representative	Estate attorney	Accountant
Financial planner/advisor	Real Estate broker	Appraiser
Auction/Estate Liquidator	Charity	Hauler

☐ Set a date to empty the house.

NOTES:

_____

_____

_____

_____

_____

_____

_____

_____

_____

_____

_____

_____

_____

_____

_____

_____

_____

_____

_____

LOCATING CRITICAL PAPERWORK

Ideally, you have gotten all paperwork organized and accounted for, but in so many situations, this is not the case. What follows is a list of what needs to be accumulated in order to best deal with your parents' estate:

- ☐ Will
- ☐ Investment statements
- ☐ Life insurance policies
- ☐ Homeowner's insurance
- ☐ Automobile insurance
- ☐ Safe combination
- ☐ Credit card information
- ☐ Last wishes
- ☐ Power of attorney
- ☐ Credit bureau reports
- ☐ Long-term care policy
- ☐ Automobile deeds / keys
- ☐ Bank account information
- ☐ Safety deposit keys
- ☐ Social security info
- ☐ Computer passwords
- ☐ Healthcare Power of Attorney
- ☐ Net worth statement
- ☐ Disability insurance papers
- ☐ Automobile bill of sale
- ☐ Retirement account info
- ☐ Real estate documents
- ☐ Driver's license
- ☐ Address book

Knowing all the people who may have assisted your parents with the above paperwork may help you locate it.

- ☐ Banker
- ☐ In-home care professional
- ☐ Accountant
- ☐ Veterinarian (if have pets)
- ☐ Financial planner
- ☐ Close friends
- ☐ Estate Planner
- ☐ Doctor(s)
- ☐ Clergyman/Pastor
- ☐ Insurance agent

Important papers are often stashed in unusual places. Consider these locations when going through the home in search of paperwork and important documents.

- ☐ Under or in mattresses
- ☐ Books or Family Bible
- ☐ Above cabinet, cornice
- ☐ Closets
- ☐ Kitchen drawers
- ☐ Mixed in with stationery
- ☐ Behind/in picture frames
- ☐ Bottom of dresser drawers
- ☐ Sort through attic
- ☐ Unmarked boxes
- ☐ Organizer containers
- ☐ Mixed in or inside greeting cards
- ☐ Behind stove or refrigerator
- ☐ Inside journals
- ☐ Freezer
- ☐ Garage
- ☐ Luggage compartments

A compilation checklist is located in Section V of this manual to help you organize all of the above items and information as you begin this daunting process.

Sentimental Journey

This is going to be a difficult task. Going through your parents' stuff will bring back memories and emotions will be high. Use these steps to make it easier and as stress-free as possible under the circumstances:

- Call a meeting among immediate siblings and heirs only.

- Contact executor and attorney.

- Contact close relatives, but keep a polite distance until immediate siblings have a strategy and know how to proceed. They can be involved a little later in the process.

- Gather sentimental items – note which are mentioned in will.

- The executor should have a home inventory and personal property appraisal conducted prior to anything leaving the house. This is to make sure all items are accounted for and they get divided fairly.

- The executor should impose a "no feuding" rule.

- Create individual wish lists among all family members for comparison.

Celebrate the life of the parent through listening to their favorite music, sharing stories, or stopping to look through family pictures.

Section IV

Cleaning Out
the House

WHAT TO DO BEFORE YOU BEGIN

You should do the following actions before you move anything or give away anything.

- ☐ An inventory of personal property should be done first to identify all the contents.
- ☐ Consider hiring a personal property appraiser to ascertain what has value vs. what does not. Think "equitable distribution."
- ☐ Keys should be retrieved and locks should be changed. This is the responsibility of the executor.
- ☐ Establish ownership of items. Do any items in the home belong to Aunt Mary, or the neighbor, or a good friend?
- ☐ Has the Will/Trust been located? Are you under direction from an attorney? If so, please follow him/her.
- ☐ If there are any specific bequests in the will or final documents, they should be filled before others become involved. For example, Mary gets mom's pearl necklace.

IF YOU HAVE NOT YET DISTRIBUTED ESTATE CONTENTS AMONG THE HEIRS

Once you have permission from the attorney to move forward and begin with the selection and division of personal property from the estate, it must be done so methodically, not permitting everyone to come over at one time. This will create chaos, tensions will be high, and it will be much harder than it has to be. Immediate heirs only go first.

Ask immediate heirs if they would put together a "wish list" of what they would like to have. This list is not a guarantee they will get what they want, but a starting place where the executor can get a professional appraiser to valuate the items on each person's list, or discover other items in the home that have value. This process should be based on equitable distribution and the best method to be fair and objective to all involved. For more practical solutions to the relational issues in an estate, please read Julie's book, *"How to Divide Your Family's Estate and Heirlooms Peacefully & Sensibly."*

If an item(s) was listed to be distributed to a certain heir(s) in the loved one's final documents, and it is in writing, this should be done before any other selections take place. Honor the loved one's wishes as best you can.

Once the immediate heirs have selected, then bring in grandchildren and extended family. Then, if mom or dad had a best friend, ask if they would like a small memento to remember them by. Sometimes it is best for the family to select a small piece for the friend or neighbor or caregiver, but use discretion.

It is human nature to take a mile if given only an inch. Even those with the best intentions lose sight of clarity during this time and will often take far more than you expect.

These are the steps you begin with to clean out the home. This process will leave the home feeling lighter and give you the available space you need for the next phase.

Once these items are selected, a date to remove the items *must* be set and everyone is responsible for moving their items by that date, no later. The executor should oversee this day(s) so no one takes advantage or takes additional items that could cause tension and feuding among heirs.

After the items have been removed, the estate now contains only items that will be sold, discarded, or donated.

IF YOU HAVE ALREADY DISTRIBUTED ESTATE CONTENTS AMONG THE HEIRS/BENEFICIARIES

If you've already distributed the family items, the next step is to establish what needs to be sold, what needs to be donated (see page 47), and what should be discarded. You can find additional information on the comparisons of selling options on page 49.

If you've put into practice everything advised thus far, you've really gotten the hardest work behind you. The emotional and physical strain that goes with settling your parents' affairs is almost done, and all that's left is rolling up your sleeves and tackling the stuff. There's something about backbreaking labor that keeps our emotions at bay.

You are a few days away from being finished with the last difficult phase of clearing out the family home. As with any task, if you have the right system for clearing out an estate, the process will go much more smoothly.

Here's what should have already taken place:

1. Remove from the house any and all property that has been divided among the heirs. Make sure everyone has removed all that they were granted. This will offer more room for you to work in the home.

2. Have all valuables or perceived valuables already identified. What should be remaining in the home are leftovers from what the heirs did not want. These are either for an estate sale or auction, or to be packed up for donation or consignment. If the heirs do not want the valuables, or there are no heirs, an estate sale professional will liquidate the contents and may clear out the home for you at an additional cost.

3. Consult with an estate professional to see what you should clean out. Some liquidators prefer you leave it as-is and will handpick what should go into the sale and pack up the rest for donation, but you may want to go through everything first. If you are cleaning out the home yourself, do not proceed until these three things are done.

NOTES:

_____

_____

_____

_____

_____

_____

_____

_____

_____

_____

_____

_____

SUPPLIES NEEDED FOR CLEANING OUT THE HOUSE

- ❑ Work clothes — jeans and a long sleeve shirt

- ❑ Good working leather gloves

- ❑ Respirator or disposable dust masks (found in paint section of hardware store)

- ❑ Kneepads for all the time spent on hands and knees

- ❑ Velcro back support for all the twisting, bending, and reaching

- ❑ Tools: screwdrivers (flat and Phillips), pliers, measuring tape, hammer

- ❑ Bug spray

- ❑ Insect bombs for attic and basement—use one week prior to going in

- ❑ At least six large rolls of packing tape

- ❑ Permanent markers for labeling boxes

- ❑ Box of 100 heavy duty black garbage bags – buy quality bags

- ❑ Forty to sixty boxes, may be more or less, depending on the estate

- ❑ Snacks and beverages (water, Gatorade) to keep everyone energized and hydrated

- ❑ Smaller boxes to hold small items

- ❑ Disposable latex gloves

- ❑ Hand truck – preferably the type with a strap to hold larger things when moving them

- ❑ Wheelbarrow – for carting large trash bags to the curb or dumpster

- ❑ Truck or van for hauling

- ❑ First aid kit

- ❑

PREPARING FOR CLEAN OUT

After a date is set and the task of cleaning out is underway, the real work begins. Eighty percent of the contents of most estates are a combination of donation or being discarded. To get things started, do the following to prepare for the clean out:

☐ Contact a local refuse company to let them know additional trash will be placed at the curb. Ask how they can help you.

☐ Contact a debris or rubbish-hauling company, or hire a dumpster.

☐ Research charities that will accept and pick up donations. Select organization(s) to receive things you'll donate. Call two or three weeks in advance. Ask if they will move the larger furniture. Reconfirm the specific date and time more than once as the pick-up date approaches.

☐ Know the location of county or municipal recycling center. Much of what you are discarding can also be recycled. Let's keep things out of the landfill, if possible.

☐ Be green by consulting with refuse haulers and local environmental agencies for the proper disposal of batteries, cleaning solvents, paint, etc. Keep these things out of the landfill too.

☐ Research and call a professional shredding company for important personal, medical, or financial documents that the executor no longer needs.

☐ Establish three collection areas: to keep; to donate; to discard.

☐ Be safe using gloves, dust masks, insect spray, ladders, and hand tools to protect from injury and properly handle the clean out.

☐ Wear jeans and a long-sleeved shirt. Even if you're cleaning the estate in the warmer months, avoid wearing shorts. This will avoid unnecessary cuts and abrasions, and act as a protective layer against pests who will bite, like spiders.

☐ Good strong workers are necessary for this work. If you need extra help, you may need to enlist some college- or high school students. If you have any health issues, please hire someone to do this work for you.

☐ Arrange for a handyman to come in as soon as the house is empty.

☐ Once the handyman is finished, arrange for a professional maid service to come in and clean thoroughly.

LET'S TALK ABOUT PAPER.

☐ Believe it or not, paper products could actually account for the bulk of the weight you have to move. It is not unusual to find tons of paper in an estate, especially if the occupant was an elderly person. Newspapers, financial statements, health care documents, magazines, catalogs, pamphlets, brochures, etc.

☐ Assign one or two people to sort through all the paper you find throughout the entire home. Papers that are necessary for the executor or power of attorney should be placed in a special box and given to them to sort through and safeguard.

☐ Documents that contain financial information that are no longer needed, Social Security numbers, etc. should be placed in trash bags and labeled with a big tag ("SHRED THIS BAG") to take to a shredding company to be destroyed appropriately.

☐ All papers should be sorted through for peace of mind.

☐ Remember to recycle. Cut down cardboard boxes and neatly stack newspapers, magazines, etc. in manageable piles so you can bag them and take them to recycle, or place them in the recycle bin at the home.

WHAT ABOUT ALL THOSE PHOTOS?

It is one of the most common questions and complaints I hear from clients: "What are we supposed to do with all these photographs of people we don't even know?"

☐ Sort through them to identify who you know.

☐ Ask other older family members if they can help in identifying any other people in the photos. Sadly, most of the time the only people who can help identify these photos are already deceased.

☐ When distributing and selecting which photos family would like to keep, remember that we live in an age when photographic reproduction is very easy. Try not to argue over an antique photo, but offer to have quality reproductions made.

☐ You can also have a CD made up of all the photos you would like to have. You can keep it all on one CD instead of hundreds of loose photos. Some like this option because it takes up less space.

☐ For the remainder of photos that are not selected by anyone, families will usually dispose of them.

GET FAMILIAR WITH THE "LAY OF THE LAND"

☐ Start with a walk-through: check every room, the attic, basement, garage, and any storage sheds. While doing this, open each closet, drawer, cabinet, cupboard, etc.

☐ Have a notepad on hand to write down unique challenges, if any. For example, is there an aquarium or very large piece of furniture that will require professional assistance?

☐ Designate rooms. Select two rooms that can be used to collect certain items. If the family has already removed what they wanted from the home, these rooms can be designated to collect *donation items* and *for-sale items.*

☐ If the family has not yet moved what they want from the estate, one room can be designated as the *safe room.* This room can be used as a temporary home for anything of value that may be found and will be kept for family later, or sold at the estate sale, but its fate is not yet decided.

☐ The next room is the *donation room.* If you decide not to conduct a sale or auction, these items will need to be boxed up and donated. Arrange for a donation company that will come and pick up at the estate. One less thing for you to do. Remember to box up these items the best you can to make donation pick-up much easier.

☐ The remainder of the home can be used to place items that will go to the estate sale, auction, or consignment. See pages 49-53 for *What's the Best Method for You? A Comparison of Options for Selling the Contents.*

☐ Make notes on any safety issues: electrical, fire hazards, loose floorboards in the attic, rickety stairs going down into the basement. Please prevent injury by having these items resolved before you begin clean out, if possible.

☐ For attics: Set off a bug bomb a week ahead of time because most attics will have wasps, hornets, bees, and spiders that can make working up there unpleasant. If you suspect rodents, such as mice or rats, are in the attic, arrange to have a professional exterminator come to the house at least several days prior to the clean out.

☐ Remove any tripping hazards like throw rugs, electrical cords, etc.

☐ During the clean out, work in teams - there's strength in numbers.

☐ Communicate with the helpers what the designated rooms are for.

☐ Plan to work two people to a room, side by side. One pulls things out; the other packs it up or runs it to one of the designated areas.

- ☐ No more than 6 people in the home, maximum. When there are more than six people in the house, then everyone starts getting confused as to what goes where, or gets in each other's way.

- ☐ Depending on the layout of the house, plan to start on the top floor and work your way down. Otherwise, you can start in the most challenging rooms first, if you want to put behind you the most arduous rooms. This option has its pros and cons. Doing the most difficult room first can be very discouraging, tiring, and drive you to a bit of madness. It can and will take the wind out of your sails. ("What the heck were they thinking, keeping all of this?")

- ☐ A typical American kitchen can be very deceiving and can take many hours to clean out. Better than 80% of what you pull out will not have been used in decades.

- ☐ Of course, other rooms may pose a much larger challenge than the kitchen, like the garage, attic, or basement.

- ☐ The advantage in doing the most arduous room first is that the hardest part is behind you. You will also have a better grasp on the time constraints for the remainder of the clean out. From a mental perspective, you will feel a satisfaction in doing the worst part first. The rest can now be done with much less effort than the hardest room.

- ☐ Finally, make sure you have your designated areas cleaned out to prepare for donation boxes and sell items. Assemble several boxes ahead of time to save time.

NOTES:

_____

_____

_____

_____

_____

_____

_____

_____

_____

THE STEP-BY-STEP CLEAN OUT PROCESS

STEP 1: THE ATTIC

- ☐ The attic gets emptied first, if there is one. Work your way downward and the flow of movement will be easier.
- ☐ Three or four people are needed to clean the attic. Like an assembly line, one person hands things down from the attic. One strong and steady person stays on the ladder, so you don't have to keep climbing up and down. One or two people running the items to the designated rooms (donate, sell, keep, or discard).
- ☐ Sometimes an attic will have a strategically placed window to throw things right into a dumpster below.
- ☐ Most of what is found in an attic will be discarded to the curb, broken down and recycled (like old cardboard boxes and magazines) or sent to donation if the items are savable.
- ☐ Caution: Search the nooks and crannies of the rafters and dark corners. Jewelry and gold coins, etc. are often tucked away up there, so please be thorough in your search. Regretfully, there might also be items of value that have suffered the extreme temperature changes and the damage is permanent.

STEP 2: THE BASEMENT

- ☐ This is the one exception to the "work from the top down" rule. If there is a basement in the home, the attic and basement may be the two most overwhelming rooms in terms of carrying items up and down.
- ☐ Whichever area appears most challenging, consider doing that area first. Get the hardest part done and out of the way.
- ☐ Three or four people will also be needed for the basement. Two of them to keep passing items up, and the other two to bring the items and immediately place them in the designated donate, sell, keep, or discard rooms.
- ☐ Try your best to send items to the most appropriate areas as quickly as possible without allowing things to pile up and create an even larger mess.
- ☐ Another option for items to be discarded: If you are working in the attic or basement, you can leave all the items to be discarded in that area until the very end,

after all the better items have been removed. Depending on how much room you have in that area, you can bag up the garbage at the very end and bring outside to the curb, the dumpster, or to be hauled away by an individual or company.

STEP 3: CLOSETS, DRESSER DRAWERS, ANYWHERE CLOTHING OR FABRIC ITEMS ARE FOUND

☐ Arrange for two people in each room to work as a team, starting with all the clothing, towels, sheets, washcloths, anything made out of cloth.

☐ Have each team of two people begin by packing the clothing, shoes, and linens.

☐ If you have only one team, do one bedroom at a time to completion, then move on to the next bedroom. Jumping around from room to room will only cause confusion and frustration.

☐ In some estates, the amount of clothing is astounding and the task is not an easy one. Also, surviving family members generally do not want to keep much of it. If it's in good shape and usable, the best thing to do with used clothing and linens is to donate them to a homeless shelter, charity, or church.

☐ Prepare each room with boxes already assembled and ready to fill, along with rolls of tape, permanent markers, etc. Box everything neatly and place all these boxes in the donation room.

☐ It is wise to select a charity that has the capacity to send a truck to the home, where they can just load it up and take it away.

STEP 4: BATHROOMS

☐ The next rooms to tackle are the bathrooms. Clear off the counters, under the sink, and in the drawers.

☐ Dispose of personal toiletries, medicine, first aid items, old heating pads, ice packs, etc. Do not flush or throw out prescription medications. Call your local pharmacist for proper disposal.

☐ Helpful hint: Do not allow the large trash bags to just sit there full and trip someone. Take turns removing them from the home, and take them to the curb two at a time. Call waste management in your city to see what they will pick up at the curb, or you may have to order a dumpster.

☐ Even though bathrooms are generally fairly small, they make a great place to store additional boxes for donation – in the shower stall or bathtub.

☐ Household chemicals and cleaning products should be given away to neighbors, friends, etc. The remainder should go to the proper chemical dump site, so they don't end up in the landfill. Some charities also take chemicals and paints.

STEP 5: ALL SMALLER ITEMS SUCH AS BRIC-A-BRAC AND DECORATIVE ITEMS

☐ After the bathrooms, concentrate on all the decorative items and knick-knacks throughout the home. Just sweep through each room and remove or pack tabletop items, shelves, curios, etc.

☐ Make sure at all times you have at least three boxes and one roll of tape near you. Place all of these knick-knacks in these boxes. Put in the donation room if they will be donated, or the designated area for items to be sold, until a professional can look at them and advise.

STEP 6: KITCHEN CABINETS, CUPBOARDS, STORAGE AREAS

☐ Kitchen: Often the kitchen is one of the more challenging rooms in the house. The best way to clean out the kitchen is with the fewest number of people possible (two is recommended) to avoid tripping over one another and allow enough space for each to work freely. Assemble boxes ahead of time, and make sure you have plenty of newspaper to pack breakable items for donation.

☐ Pantry: Get rid of the expired canned goods first. The two people can box up any canned goods or food items that are still within the expiration date. Label each box to take to the local soup kitchen, religious organization, or shelter. All perishables and expired food need to be thrown out immediately. If you are unsure of the expiration date, throw it out. Most spices are usually too old to save.

☐ Cabinets: Next, the same two people will handle all the glassware. If family members or friends can use these items for college-age kids, etc. distribute to them as quickly as possible. If not, donate these items.

☐ Glassware and Glass Jars: You will find an inexplicable amount of glasses and glassware, both in sets and many that are mismatched. Sets can be sold if you wish, but odd glasses should be donated. Glass mayonnaise jars, baby food jars, peanut butter jars, etc. should be set aside to be recycled. The same goes for the multitude of pie tins and foil you will find.

- ☐ <u>Plastic containers</u>: Throw out or recycle all plastic containers, Cool Whip containers, margarine tubs, old Tupperware, etc. Discard them, because plastic is known for breeding bacteria.
- ☐ <u>Pots and Pans</u>: Old pots and pans that are mismatched should either be donated or sent to scrap metal. If some of the cookware is supposed to come with an electric cord that is lost, or the pots are too old, let them go. Pyrex and Corning Ware usually sell well at estate sales as long as they are in good condition.
- ☐ <u>China/Dishes/Crystal/Silver</u>: If your mother had sets of china, crystal, or silver, it may be worthwhile putting the sets in a sale or sending to auction. Try to keep them together as sets.
- ☐ <u>Small appliances</u>: Donate or sell countertop appliances such as coffee makers, electric can openers, mixers, and microwaves, if in good enough condition to sell and if they are not too old. If not, donate these items.

STEP 7: BEDROOMS

- ☐ Now that you have already cleaned out the closets, drawers, and smaller decorative items, what should be left in each bedroom is furniture, TV, men's valet stand, chair and ottoman, or settee.
- ☐ <u>If you are having an estate sale</u>: If there are enough items to warrant an estate sale or some kind of family sale, leave the furniture right where it is and tag it "to be sold." On the day of the sale, customers will want to inspect the furniture, so don't disassemble it or move it. The estate sale professional will do that. Save yourself some extra work by leaving heavy pieces right where they are.
- ☐ <u>If you are donating</u>: If you decide to donate these furniture pieces, disassemble the beds and mattresses, remove mirrors from dressers, etc. Place them along the wall to make more room. Find a charity that will do the moving for you, and leave the pieces in each bedroom, if possible.

STEP 8: GARAGE AND OUTDOOR SHEDS

- ☐ Hand tools, yard equipment, power tools, lawn mowers/tractors, are definitely sellable if in good condition.
- ☐ You will find many things hidden in garages. Glass jars filled with all kinds of screws, nails, nuts and bolts, chemicals galore. Extension cords often need to be discarded due to damage or wear. Ladders can be kept by family or sold. The same is true for wheelbarrows and garden supplies.

☐ The men in the family like to sort through the tools. Donate or sell the leftovers.

☐ Be careful when cleaning out garages and outdoor sheds. Purchase bug bombs and use about a week ahead of time to kill insects. Remember to wear long sleeves, boots, and long jeans.

STEP 9: UNIQUE CHALLENGES

☐ In every estate, there are a couple of unique situations you may not be sure how to handle. Perhaps the estate has a piano or other very heavy piece, like an aquarium. Perhaps the doorways are too narrow to accommodate moving an item easily.

☐ Take notes of these special items and document what the problem is. When you run into a situation where you just don't know what to do, call a time-out break and get everyone's input. Ask family members, colleagues, etc. It may be time to arrange for specialists to come in and handle those particular items.

WHAT IF WE FIND SOMETHING OF SIGNIFICANT VALUE?

☐ When it comes to clearing out every room and closet, be thorough and anticipate some hidden valuables. Loved ones from the Depression Era have a long-term distrust of banks and often hid valuables in the strangest places.

☐ If you uncover a collection of gold coins, rare baseball cards, diamonds, jewelry, etc. please notify the executor immediately and document all that you found.

☐ The next step is to have these items looked at by a professional personal property appraiser. It is worth the cost to hire them to ascertain what has value versus what doesn't have value.

☐ Once value has been determined, the item(s) can either be sold and proceeds split between heirs, an heir can offer to buy it outright from the estate with the estate's permission, or it can be donated to a museum, for example.

☐ Always take the high road and report back to the family what was found.

ALZHEIMER'S AND MEMORY IMPAIRMENT

☐ Leave no stone unturned. With this particular disease, the chance for things missing is very high. The optimal prevention for this challenge is to secure the valuables prior to the disease progressing to the extent that they are either giving things away or throwing them away.

☐ With many types of dementia, paranoia has a play and our loved one may get frightful and start hiding items. Unfortunately, they forget where they put these items; you must be the detective. Family members may jump to the conclusion that these items have been stolen or given away. That might very well be the case, but it is also possible that these items are well hidden.

THE PERSONAL BENEFIT OF CLEANING OUT AN ESTATE

☐ You will be amazed at the variety of emotions you will go through as you clean out an estate. You might experience anger, frustration, and bewilderment as to why they kept all the stuff they did. These feelings are normal and usually strike when you're right in the middle of the most difficult room, or as you carry bag after bag to the curb. "Mom, why did you keep all this stuff? What were you thinking? Why did you leave it all for us to clean up?"

☐ Please recognize the benefit in this situation. You may vow to never do this to your children and let things get to this level. You will remind yourself to go through closets routinely and donate all that you no longer need, want, etc.

☐ Look closely at your collecting habits and stop the bad ones. Did you know we regularly use about 20 percent of what we own? The other 80 percent that we don't use is just sitting in our closets, garages, and attics.

☐ It is encouraging to see the downsizing and simplicity trends coming from today's boomers and the younger generations. Make yourself a promise: Whatever is brought into the house, two things will have to leave and find a new home.

NOTES:

_____

_____

_____

_____

_____

_____

_____

FINDING EVERYTHING

Finding valuable and items of sentimental value to your parents may not be in the most likely places, especially if they suffered from dementia or Alzheimer's. Leave no pillow unturned and no drawer unopened. Here are some likely stashing places:

- ☐ Pockets of coats or jackets
- ☐ Container in freezer or refrigerator
- ☐ Inside books, greetings cards
- ☐ Attic rafters or basement crawl spaces
- ☐ Outbuilding or barn
- ☐ Inside socks or wrapped in underwear
- ☐ Trunks in attic or storage
- ☐ Toilet tanks
- ☐ Bra cups
- ☐ Ice cube trays
- ☐ Gift bags, holiday wrapping paper
- ☐ Beneath floor boards
- ☐ Taped under desk drawers

- ☐ Purses, wallets, suit cases
- ☐ Canister sets
- ☐ Wrapped in duct tape (coins, jewelry)
- ☐ Loose floor boards
- ☐ Inside old cardboard jewelry boxes
- ☐ Plastic containers (Cool Whip, margarine)
- ☐ Shoe liners, coat liners
- ☐ Inside or under mattress
- ☐ Drapery hems, sofa cushions
- ☐ Garbage bag boxes
- ☐ Inside photo frames behind image
- ☐ Tool or fishing tackle boxes

NOTES:

_____

_____

_____

_____

_____

_____

_____

_____

_____

_____

_____

CLEANING OUT DO'S AND DON'TS

To follow are the Do's and Don'ts I have learned for preparing to clean out family homes. Use this as a guide for you and your family as well.

DO's

☐ Do keep only what is special to you (not what you think 2 generations from now might desire – chances are they won't want much).

☐ Do choose wisely. Not everything in the home is sentimental.

☐ Do the right thing always. Be ethical and fair.

☐ Do hire a personal property appraiser to evaluate the estate contents prior to division of property. The executor should place emphasis on valuables in order to divide the contents equitably. It is well worth the fee for this objective third party to assist you with values and produce a document for future use.

☐ Do communicate with other heirs that there will be no fighting during the cleaning out phase of the estate.

☐ Do have family meetings leading up to the cleaning of the estate with some set guidelines.

☐ Do share. If you find anything, place it on the dining table and share with siblings, like mom's long lost diamond, special documents from dad's war days, anything you feel is of importance.

☐ Do honor your parents the best that you can. It is not always 100% possible, but try your best so you can have a clear conscience.

☐ Do turn the other cheek with your siblings. Frequently.

☐ Do speak your mind. If something bothers you, it's ok to talk about it and share, but don't push your opinion on everyone else. Speak, then listen to possible solutions and be open to them.

☐ Do preserve family history if at all possible.

☐ Do utilize the electronic age – scan photographs and documents for everybody

☐ Do keep "sets" as sets. Don't divide necklace and matching earrings. Keep it together.

☐ Do set clear boundaries for neighbors and friends that want too much. This goes for relatives, too.

- ☐ Do alert police and neighbors to a vacant home.
- ☐ Do keep utilities on (water and electricity).
- ☐ Do keep good care of yourself: stay hydrated, take vitamins, and eat/sleep well.
- ☐ Do an inventory of existing supplies already in the house before you go buy more.
- ☐ Do retrieve all keys to the property.
- ☐ Do cancel newspapers and re-route mail.
- ☐ Do find out garbage day right away.
- ☐ Do recycle as much as possible.
- ☐ Do empty refrigerator as soon as possible.

NOTES:

_____

_____

_____

_____

_____

_____

_____

_____

_____

_____

_____

_____

_____

_____

_____

_____

DON'TS

☐ Don't fight, disrespect or dishonor. For every problem, there is a solution.

☐ Don't hide anything from other siblings or heirs.
   Always put it out on the table for everyone to see, whether it is a material possession, or a valuable item, or a problem. Hiding raises suspicion and harbors resentment.

☐ Don't take things just to have them.
   Heirs often make the error of taking too much, and this can cause marital strife and hard feelings among other family members. Usually two years afterward, you will question why you took so much and want to sell it.

☐ Don't take things on the premise that your kids or grandkids will want them later.
   The younger generation is not interested in china, crystal or old sofas. They want IKEA, Pottery Barn, Crate and Barrel. Select carefully for them.

☐ Don't ever let a material possession come between you and a loved one.

☐ Don't take so much that your children will have this burden one day.

☐ Don't stuff everything in storage.
   The intent to keep things stored for a short while is genuine; but often, stuff remains there for years on end. Storage costs can become a financial burden too. No one really wants to deal with it or has room for it in their own homes. If you don't have room for it now, chances are you won't in the future either.

☐ Don't store valuables that can be damaged.

☐ Don't keep antiques in the attic. The attic is the worst place for valuables.

☐ Don't feel obliged to take it just because it was your parents.

☐ Don't be fooled. All that glitters is not gold.

☐ Don't hesitate to hire a professional to do this for you. Check references.

☐ Don't rush through an estate so you miss something important

☐ Don't take so long to go through the estate that it takes over your life.

☐ Don't forget neighbors and friends who were important to your parents.

☐ Don't forget to secure the property

☐ Don't let financial or healthcare information end up in the trash. Shred it.

☐ Don't throw anything away or donate it until you know the value.

☐ Don't get rid of computer until all personal information is erased or deleted.

☐ Don't assume it is junk. One person's junk is another person's treasure.

KEEP, SELL, OR DONATE

I always advise my clients to keep what is truly special to them. For some heirs, whatever items have monetary value are what they want to keep, often with the next generation in mind, or to sell on their own for cash. It is important to note that the younger generations rarely desire some of the antique or older items that may be in grandmother's home and this should be taken into consideration, as the storage of these items may be difficult for years to come.

For others, it is about the sentimental items that connect special memories directly to your heart. It might be family photographs, a pair of grandma's spectacles or dad's war medals.

What you decide to keep is completely dependent on what you have always treasured from the family or home. Remember that you cannot keep it all and you don't want to leave a burden for your heirs, so choose wisely and try to keep it as simple as possible.

WHAT'S IMPORTANT ENOUGH TO KEEP OR CONSIDER KEEPING

Temporarily keep it all until items in the home have been evaluated by a professional and the family can make educated decisions on whether to keep them or sell.

- ☐ Anything that can provide family history.
- ☐ Family heirlooms.
- ☐ Evaluate all items of perceived monetary value (hire appraiser too).
- ☐ Some family photographs. (More on this in the next section).
- ☐ Items that are considered heirlooms IF someone has room for them and wants them. It's ok to sell if no one wants them.
- ☐ Jewelry - have it appraised first.
- ☐ Items with historic significance - may donate if you wish.
- ☐ Important documents must be kept together until they are all sorted through by the executor.
- ☐ Collections: gold, coins, guns, stamps, etc. Always have them evaluated by a professional.
- ☐ Antiques, artwork - paintings, sculptures - must be evaluated by a professional.

☐ Military items.

☐ Safes, safety deposit boxes, and their contents.

☐ Anything you cannot identify.

WHAT TO DO WITH OLD FAMILY PHOTOS NO ONE CAN IDENTIFY

If the last remaining family member who can identify the people in the photos has died, you have three options:

☐ Distribute them and eventually someone will dispose of them,

☐ Dispose of them now. It is shame that so many go unidentified because our family history often dies with our parents' generation.

☐ Some antique photos can be sold particularly if they have antique frames. Decorators and collectors have interest.

WHAT IF YOU WANT TO KEEP ITEMS BUT DON'T HAVE THE ROOM

Take photos and keep a digital memory file. It takes up less space and then the item can be given away or sold.

NOTE: **More on what to keep can be found in** *How to Divide Your Family's Estate and Heirlooms Peacefully and Sensibly,* **also by Julie Hall.**

NOTES:

_____

_____

_____

_____

_____

_____

_____

WHAT TO SELL IF NO ONE IN THE FAMILY WANTS IT:

In all of the following cases, be sure you know the real value, especially of collectibles and unique items. Never assume anything. What you think has value and what actually does is best left to those who do this for a living. Hiring a personal property appraiser will give you answers, knowledge, and peace of mind, prior to selling.

- ☐ Furniture
- ☐ Silver
- ☐ Electronics
- ☐ Furs
- ☐ Knick-knacks
- ☐ Vehicles
- ☐ Hobby items/supplies
- ☐ Mirrors
- ☐ China and crystal
- ☐ Linens
- ☐ Vintage clothing
- ☐ Seasonal/Holiday items
- ☐ Recreational items
- ☐ Artwork
- ☐ Kitchenware
- ☐ Tools/garden items
- ☐ Decorator items
- ☐ Appliances
- ☐ Sporting goods

ANTIQUE, VINTAGE, COLLECTIBLE?

These terms are often misunderstood and improperly used. When determining the value of any item, it is always best to consult a professional appraiser.

- ☐ Antique refers to an item that is at least one hundred years old.

- ☐ Vintage describes older items that are not yet one hundred years old. Generally, vintage items are seen in antique stores and considered collectible. Vintage pieces are original to the period that produced them and not reproductions.

- ☐ Collectible refers to anything people collect, usually older items on their way to becoming antique.

NOTES:

_____

_____

_____

_____

_____

_____

_____

Collectibles, Vintage & Antique Items

You should have any of these items reviewed by a professional appraiser to determine value:

Advertising signs or posters
Artwork (signed, original)
    Paintings, lithographs, etc
B Barbie dolls

Baseball cards/sports memorabilia
Black Americana
Books (first editions and leather-bound)
Cameras / photographic equipment
Christmas items
Clothing (vintage/designer)

Coin and stamp collections
Cookie jars
Crystal (antique/signed)
Dolls and accessories
Early electric fans
Fishing lures
Fountain pens
Furniture
European figurines
    Especially German and English
Glassware
Guns
Inkwells
Jewelry
Kitchenware
Lace or crochet work
Ladies Compacts

Lamps
Linens
Lionel trains (original)
Mantel clocks / long case clocks
Movie posters
Paperweights (signed)
Perfumes
Photos
Pocket watches (railroad. old)
    (gold)
Porcelain ware
Post cards
Primitives (folk art)
Quilts
Radios
Railroad memorabilia
Rugs (oriental)
Sculptures
Smoking collectibles
Sterling silver, gold, platinum
Tapestries
Tools
Toys
War memorabilia

WHAT TO DONATE

Anything you or the heirs do not want, can't use, or you decide to forego having in a liquidation sale, would be appreciated by those less fortunate. In some cases, once items have been divided and distributed, there is not enough to conduct a liquidation sale. I often advise clients that donation is a wonderful option in lieu of selling the small amount of remaining items that the family does not want.

Items you donate are also tax deductible. Your accountant should be able to advise you for your situation. Items worthy of donating include:

☐ Clothing of all kinds: shoes, coats, suits, etc.

☐ Linens, towels, bed sheets, etc.

☐ Older upholstered or wood furniture: sofas, dining furniture, bookcases, chairs.

☐ Electronics, computers, telephones.

☐ Non-perishable food for shelters, if before the expiration date.

☐ Tools and equipment.

☐ Kitchenware.

☐ Craft supplies.

☐ Durable medical equipment like wheelchairs, walkers, canes.

    Note: Personal medical equipment like respiratory aids can not be donated.

☐ Prescription eye glasses.

☐ Office equipment and supplies.

☐ Books and magazines.

NOTES:

_____

_____

_____

_____

_____

_____

_____

WHO TO DONATE TO:

- ☐ Local community charities.
- ☐ Shelters (homeless, battered women, etc.).
- ☐ Faith-based organizations/ministries.
- ☐ Food Banks.
- ☐ Hospice.
- ☐ Local veterinarians (often need towels, etc.).
- ☐ Local Alzheimer's facilities (some need bed sheets and linens).
- ☐ Goodwill Industries
- ☐ Salvation Army
- ☐ Kidney Foundation
- ☐ Crisis Assistance organizations
- ☐ Habitat for Humanity
- ☐ Shriners collect old eyeglasses, or can be dropped off at eye doctor office

NOTES:

_____

_____

_____

_____

_____

_____

_____

_____

_____

_____

_____

_____

_____

WHAT'S THE BEST METHOD FOR YOU?

A Comparison of Options for Selling the Contents

When considering the most appropriate methods of liquidation for the estate, do your homework and talk with different professionals, and friends or colleagues that have gone through the process. No two estates are alike. While one might fare much better with an upper tier auction house, another will do exceptionally well with an estate sale onsite. If you only have a handful of pieces to sell, consignment might be the best option. There are many factors that will influence the most appropriate method for you to choose.

The options available to you are consignment, doing it yourself, using an auction house, or hiring an estate sales professional. Here are overviews of each including pros and cons to help you make the best decision for your unique situation.

CONSIGNMENT:
- ☐ **Location** – Estate items will need to brought to the consignment store first to see if they are interested in them. However, some stores will come to you, view the items and let you know if they are interested in consigning some of them.
- ☐ **Duration** – Can take 90-120 days.
- ☐ **Residential Content** – Are the items what they are looking for? They like decorative items, new and antique items, nicer things, etc. They will advise you what they can and cannot sell.
- ☐ **Fees/Commission** – 40%-50%, plus often a "moving or pick up fee" that can be reasonable or quite high depending on the area and the store. Not all stores have this fee, so please ask.
- ☐ **Payment** – Payment is usually once or twice a month for the time period items are kept.
- ☐ **Set-Up Time**– They handle it all
- ☐ **Man Power** – They handle it all
- ☐ **Pricing** – The consignment will price it all and may or may not seek an appraisal on items.
- ☐ **Leftovers/Remnants** (what doesn't sell) – Depending on your contract, they either donate leftovers to charity or you can come retrieve the items. Please ask.

Consignment Pros:	Consignment Cons:
They may pick it up	You may have to take items to them
They set pricing	Pricing may not be professionally appraised
They handle all aspects of sale	Higher commission
	Additional pick up or move fee.
	They may not take all that you want to sell

DOING IT YOURSELF (DIY):

- ☐ **Location** – On-site, inside and outside – you decide
- ☐ **Duration** – This is up to you.
- ☐ **Advertising** – You will need to place appropriate ads in the local papers, make directional signs and strategically place them, as well as handle electronic notifications to the public. This may require purchasing a list, which can get expensive.
- ☐ **Residential Content** – Do you know what everything is worth and the current market value on those items? It is advisable to have this information prior to selling.
- ☐ **Fees/Commission** – Sweat equity
- ☐ **Payment** – Immediate - You retain all the proceeds to divide among heirs.
- ☐ **Set-Up Time**– You do it all: pull it out, organize it properly and in a way that will maximize proceeds.
- ☐ **Man Power** – You do it all and will need a team of people. Not everyone listens or takes direction well, especially sentimental family members.
- ☐ **Pricing** – Do you know how to appropriately price items? You may still need to hire a professional appraisal on items.
- ☐ **Leftovers/Remnants** (what doesn't sell) – Go back through it, divide it among heirs, box up and donate the remainder, pick up and fill out tax form.

DIY Pros:	DIY Cons:
You get all proceeds from sale	It is much harder than you think
	Will take much longer than you think
	Can take months, sometimes years
	Expenses in advertising and promotion
	May not price items properly
	Often children/siblings have different ideas
	Can lead to tension among family
	Takes a great deal of energy

HIRING AN AUCTION COMPANY:

- [ ] **Location** – Can take place at the auction house or at the estate if they are also selling the real property as well as the personal property. If selling personal property only, they will probably come pack it up to store at the auction house until the next scheduled auction.
- [ ] **Duration** – May take 1-3 days for the actual auction
- [ ] **Payment** - Can take well over a month or longer to get paid.
- [ ] **Advertising** – Many auction companies charge extra for this, while some include it. Auction houses typically have large lists of prospective buyers and will also use internet sites to advertise the auction. Be sure and ask.
- [ ] **Residential Content** – Is what you have to sell enough in quantity, as well as quality, for an auction company? If you have higher end items, they should go to an upper tier auction house. Average, everyday items can go to other auction houses, but are often sold in "box lots" which means several things are put into a box and sold together as a unit. These can sell for very little, but the public loves them.
- [ ] **Fees/Commission** – Typically 20-35% range of what is sold (though some may be higher or lower). Some also have a Buyer's Premium which can be an additional 10-20%. The buyer's premium' is a percentage additional charge on the hammer price of the lot. It is made by the auctioneer to cover his 'administrative expenses.' Ask about "pick up" fees of potential storage fees. Some auctions charge to pack items up and move the items back to the auction. Ask about any other hidden fees and make sure there is a contract involved with an itemization of what you are consigning to the auction company.
- [ ] **Weather** – This is not a problem if the auction is inside.
- [ ] **Set Up Time**– The ease of an auction is a benefit. They come, get it and set it up.
- [ ] **Man Power** – They take care of this for you.
- [ ] **Pricing** – An auction allows the public to decide what something will sell for, starting with a bidding price to initiate bids. The auctioneers' job is to guide the bidding process, while trying to bring in as much revenue as possible through enticing the public to bid higher. Sometimes it works on the seller's behalf, other times it works to the buyer's advantage when they get an item for a lower price than anticipated.
- [ ] **Leftovers/Remnants (what doesn't sell)** – Each auction is different; a good question for the auction you contact is to find out how they handle leftovers after the auction has taken place. Typically, after an auction, it either gets sold at some price or the consignor must pick up. If the auction is at the home-site, there is usually an additional fee for putting the home back in order and handling leftovers. Please ask questions and confirm the policy and any additional fees in advance.

Auction House Pros:

Takes place under one roof
They come and get it
They send you a check
Higher value items glean higher prices
Advertising online
A huge list of potential buyers

Auction House Cons:

Slow payment
Fees should be carefully reviewed

HIRING A PROFESSIONAL ESTATE LIQUIDATOR:

☐ **Location** – Can take place on-site at the estate or occasionally removed and sold elsewhere for a better location. Most conduct them on-site.

☐ **Duration** – Estate sales are normally conducted in 1-3 days for the actual estate sale to be completed.

☐ **Payment** - Some estate sale professionals pay you the same day, while others send you the paperwork within a few days after the estate sale, with a company check for the proceeds.

☐ **Advertising** – Some estate sale professionals charge extra for this, and some include it in their percentage. Most liquidators have a large electronic list to advertise the upcoming sale and also use estate sale sites on the internet as well. Be sure and ask.

☐ **Residential Content** – Is what you have to sell enough in quantity, as well as quality, for an estate sale professional to attract buyers to the house? If you have very high-end items, the professional should broker the items to an upper tier auction house, or advise you to do this. Sometimes an estate sale is not the correct choice, if the family takes and distributes the bulk of the estate, and not enough is left over for the professional to work with. If the bulk of the estate is to be sold, an estate sale should definitely be considered. Also, some professionals may have a "minimum" for which they will accept the sale.

☐ **Fees/Commission** – Most professionals are in the 30-40% range based on the overall sale of items (though some may be higher or lower) depending on geographical region. This commission is usually for conducting the sale only. In some cases, it might include packing up the remainders after the sale. Most liquidators will charge an additional hourly rate above their percentage to finish clearing out the home because it is difficult and time-consuming work. Ask about advertising; if the professional includes it in their percentage or if it is a separate fee.

☐ **Weather** – Sometimes weather can play havoc with an estate sale. There are those die-hard buyers who will always be there and some it might frighten away, especially winter weather, tornados, etc. Most estate sales are inside the home and the professional will try to protect the carpet/flooring.

☐ **Set-Up Time**- It takes several days or longer to properly set up for an estate sale to maximize proceeds for the client and make it look attractive for the perspective buyers.

☐ **Man Power** – A professional will use a team of two or three people to help with the set up of an average estate sale. More people will be used if the estate is large.

☐ **Pricing** – The estate sale professional sets the prices. Occasionally, the family can select two or three items in which to place a reserve price, but the professional will set the prices, because he or she will know what the market will bring in that area. Many people feel they know book value by looking a similar item up on the internet. Book value is simply not used with estate sales and no one will pay that price, unless you have something exceptionally unusual and collectable. Most of what someone has *does not* have the value we perceive it has. Each item is tagged and marked. That is the price, or the professional may negotiate but won't give it away. For the most part, he/she has control over the pricing, whereas an auction sells to the highest bidder.

☐ **Leftovers/Remnants** (what doesn't sell) – Depending on your contract, you can either ask the professional to empty the home for an additional fee and they will arrange charity and sweep before they leave. Or, you may request that the leftovers stay and you can handle the charity and emptying of the home.

Estate Liquidator Pros:

Takes place on-site
Professional will clear out
Professional will organize, set up
Maximizes proceeds
May also clear out the home
Handles all details for you
More control over pricing
Can mean higher realized prices
Payment is usually quick
Home emptied in short period of time

Estate Liquidator Cons:

Strangers coming into home
Liability insurance on property

When considering hiring a company, it is always a good idea to check the Better Business Bureau (BBB) to make sure there are no unresolved complaints. Never select a professional based on fees. Always check with local colleagues, friends, etc. and compare notes.

NOTES:

_____

_____

_____

_____

_____

_____

_____

_____

_____

_____

_____

_____

_____

Section V

Helpful
Resource Links

The Internet is a great place to look for help with specific issues relating to caring for your aging parents and liquidating their estate. Here's a list of places to start.

APPRAISALS

www.appraisers.org
American Society of Appraisers

www.isa-appraisers.org
International Society of Appraisers

DISPOSAL / RECYCLE

www.shredit.com
Shredding service

www.recycle.net
Help and resources for getting rid of junk

ELDER CARE SUPPORT

www.aarp.org
National website for the American Association of Retired Persons that provides education, advocacy, and research

www.aarp.org/drive
AARP Driver Safety Program
To locate a refresher driving program in your area

www.agenet.com
Information for the elderly, including financial, legal, health care, and other advice

www.Aging-Parents-and-Elder-Care.com
Aging Solutions — Articles, comprehensive checklists, and links to key resources designed to make it easier for people caring for an aging parent or elderly spouse to quickly find the information they need

NOTES:

www.aahsa.org   202-783-2242
American Association of Homes and Services for
the Aging (AAHSA)

www.alfa.org   703-894-1805
Assisted Living Federation of America
Consumer information on elder housing options,
services, and protections

www.agingcare.com
Resources about aging and elder care, ranging from
support with daily living to financial and legal
information as well as community support.

www.caregiverslibrary.org
National Caregivers Library

www.familycaregivers.org
Center for Family Caregivers

www.caps4caregivers.org   800-227-7294
Children of Aging Parents
Information, resources, and referrals for caregivers
of aging parents.

Eldercare Locator   800-677-1116
The Eldercare Locator can put you in contact with
the Office for the Aging in your area, which
provides help in locating needed services in your
area (a service administered by the National
Association of Area Agencies on Aging and the
National Association of State Units on Aging).

National Transit Resource Center   800-527-8279
Provides referrals for transportation for seniors

www.ec-online.net
Eldercare Online
Whether you are caring for a spouse, parent,
relative, or neighbor, this is an online community
where supportive peers and professionals help you
improve quality of life for yourself and your elder.

NOTES:

_____

_____

_____

_____

_____

_____

_____

_____

_____

_____

_____

_____

_____

_____

_____

_____

_____

_____

_____

_____

_____

_____

_____

_____

www.extendedcare.com/Search/Search.aspx
Extended Care Info Network
Detailed directory of long-term care providers, home
health agencies, retirement communities, hospices,
and nursing homes; searchable by city, county, state,
type of facility, or institution name; also lists related
Internet resources.

www.caregiving.org
National Alliance for Caregiving
Offering information, education, and support to
families caring for loved ones.

www.4fate.org
Foundation Aiding the Elderly ~ Assuring our elders
are treated with care, dignity, and the utmost respect
during their final years when they can no longer take
care of themselves

www.hospicefoundation.org   800-854-3402
Hospice Foundation of America
Information on Medicare, managed care, Medigap
insurance, long-term care insurance, long-term care
facilities, and reports on health care fraud prevention
programs

ELDER HEALTHCARE ISSUES

www.alz.org   800-272-3900
Alzheimer's Association

www.alzinfo.org
Comprehensive information about Alzheimer's
disease

www.heart.org   800-242-8721
American Heart Association
Information on heart disease as well as local chapter
information

www.cancer.org   800-227-2345
American Cancer Society

NOTES:

_____
_____
_____
_____
_____
_____
_____
_____
_____
_____
_____
_____
_____
_____
_____
_____
_____
_____
_____
_____
_____
_____
_____
_____
_____
_____

www.strokeassociation.org   888-478-7653
American Stroke Association

www.BenefitsCheckUp.org
A free, easy-to-use service that identifies federal and
state assistance programs for older
Americans

www.kff.org   202-347-5270
Kaiser Family Foundation
Talking with your parents about Medicare and
health coverage

www.webmd.com
General medical site with definitions of medical
terms and information on diseases and available
treatments

www.wellspouse.org   800-838-0879
Well Spouse Foundation
Support and resources for spousal caregivers

www.nadsa.org   877-745-1440
National Adult Day Services Association (NADSA)

www.nahc.org   202-547-7424
National Association for Home Care & Hospice
Advises on selecting a home care or hospice
provider and locates agencies in the area

www.caremanager.org
National Association of Professional Geriatric Care
Managers

www.ncal.org   202-842-4444
National Center for Assisted Living
Information on all aspects of assisted living and
residential care facilities

NOTES:

_____

_____

_____

_____

_____

_____

_____

_____

_____

_____

_____

_____

_____

_____

_____

_____

_____

_____

_____

_____

_____

_____

_____

www.theconsumervoice.org   202-332-2275
National Consumer Voice for Quality Long-Term Care

www.talkaboutrx.org   301-340-3940
National Council on Patient Information and Education
Questions to ask when taking prescription and nonprescription medicines; safe medicine use.

www.ncoa.org   202-479-1200
National Council on the Aging
Organizations and professionals dedicated to promoting the dignity, self-determination, and well-being of older persons

www.nfcacares.org   800-896-3650
National Family Caregivers Association (NFCA)

www.health.nih.gov   301-496-4000
National Institutes of Health – Seniors Health

www.nmha.org   800-969-6642
Mental Health America
Free information about mental health, mental illness, and local treatment facilities

www.parkinson.org   800-473-4636
National Parkinson Foundation
Free information, support, and local resources

www.nhcoa.org   202-347-9733
National Hispanic Council on Aging

ESTATE LIQUIDATION

www.aselonline.com
American Society of Estate Liquidators

www.auctioneers.org
National Association of Auctioneers

NOTES:

_____
_____
_____
_____
_____
_____
_____
_____
_____
_____
_____
_____
_____
_____
_____
_____
_____
_____
_____
_____
_____
_____
_____
_____
_____

FINANCIAL

www.fpanet.org
Financial Planners Association

www.centerltc.org
Center for LTC Financing
Long term care financing information, assistance, and reform.

GOVERNMENT

www.aoa.gov   202-619-0724
U.S. Administration on Aging
Elder care ideas, topics, elder abuse, LTC ombudsman.

www.seniors.gov   800-333-4636
Access to government websites and information

www.medicare.gov   800-633-4227
U.S. government site for Medicare information, including comparison of health and drug plans

www.medicare.gov/Nhcompare/Home.asp
Medicare Nursing Home Ratings
A tool that enables you to read about ratings of local nursing homes in your area

www.hhs.gov   877-696-6775
U.S. Department of Health and Human Services
Agency for protecting the health of U.S. residents

www.ncea.aoa.gov
U.S. Administration on Aging's National Center on Elder Abuse

www.ssa.gov   800-772-1213
U.S. Social Security Administration online information and resources

NOTES:

_____

_____

_____

_____

_____

_____

_____

_____

_____

_____

_____

_____

_____

_____

_____

_____

_____

_____

_____

_____

LEGAL ASSISTANCE

www.search-attorneys.com
To find an estate planning, probate, or elder law attorney

www.naela.org
National Academy of Elder Law Attorneys

www.abanet.org/aging/toolkit   202-662-1000
American Bar Association Commission on Law and Aging
Consumer's Tool Kit for Health Care Advance Planning

www.bbb.org/us/consumers
Better Business Bureau Foundation
Provides information about consumer frauds and scams, and tips for prevention

www.preventelderabuse.com
National Committee for the Prevention of Elder Abuse ~ Committed to help fight any abuse, and working to educate the public about the misuse of guardianships imposed on elders

www.ethicalwill.com
Information on creating an ethical will

ORGANIZING

www.optoutprescreen.com   888-567-8688
Stop unwanted junk mail

www.napo.net
National Association of Professional Organizers

www.elderweb.com
Locating records and property

www.nasmm.org
National Association of Senior Move Managers

NOTES:

_____
_____
_____
_____
_____
_____
_____
_____
_____
_____
_____
_____
_____
_____
_____
_____
_____
_____
_____
_____
_____
_____
_____
_____
_____

Section VI

Worksheets, Checklists & Forms

Important Information Reference Sheet

Important Document Locator List

Important People Contact List

RX Medical/Medication Checklist

Phone Notification Directory

Wish List Spreadsheet

Home Inventory List

Room by Room Walkthrough Worksheet

Donation List

Important Information

Father	Mother
Social Security Number	Social Security Number
Driver's License Number	Driver's License Number
Vehicle #1 Year/Make/Model	Vehicle #1 Year/Make/Model
Vehicle #1 VIN	Vehicle #1 VIN
Vehicle #1 Loan/Lease Account Number	Vehicle #1 Loan/Lease Account Number
Vehicle #1 Loan/Lease Contract Number	Vehicle #1 Loan/Lease Contract Number
Location of Title, if owned	Location of Title, if owned
Bank Name/Contact Info	**Account Type/Account Number**
1.	1.
2.	2.
3.	3.
4.	4.
5.	5.
Credit Card Name/Contact Info	**Account Number**
1.	1.
2.	2.
3.	3.
4.	4.
Stocks and Bonds Info	
Broker/Website	Contact Info
User Name	Password
Additional Info	

Mortgage Company	
Company Name	Account Number
Contact Info	
Any related liens?	
Insurance Company	
Life Insurance #1 Company	Life Insurance #2 Company
Life Insurance #1 Policy Number	Life Insurance #2 Policy Number
Life Insurance #1 Contact	Life Insurance #2 Contact
Health Insurance #1 Company	Health Insurance #2 Company
Health Insurance #1 Policy Number	Health Insurance #2 Policy Number
Health Insurance #1 Contact	Health Insurance #2 Contact
Home Insurance Company	
Home Insurance Policy Number	
Home Insurance Contact	
Auto Insurance #1 Company	Auto Insurance #2 Company
Auto Insurance #1 Policy Number	Auto Insurance #2 Policy Number
Auto Insurance #1 Contact	Auto Insurance #2 Contact
Login User Name	**Login Password**
Computer	
Cell Phone	
Online Banking	
OTHER	

Important Document List

DOCUMENT	LOCATION	CONTACT INFORMATION
LEGAL		
Last Will & Testament		
Living Will		
Revocable Living Trust		
Durable Power of Attorney		
FINANCIAL		
Bank Statements		
Retirement Accounts		
Loans		
Investment Accounts		
Stocks/Mutual Funds		
Life Insurance Policies		
HEALTH CARE		
Medical Records		
Current Physicians		
Signed Releases		
Health Care Power of Attorney		
Declaration for a Natural Death (Living Will)		
OTHER		
Military/Veteran's Records		
Professional Organizations/Fraternal Groups		
Real Estate		
Employment		
Education		
Appraisals for Valuables		
Personal Papers		

Important People

TYPE	NAME	CONTACT INFORMATION
Attorney		
Attorney		
Physician		
Physician		
Physician		
Financial Planner		
Insurance Agent		
Estate Planner		
Clergy (Priest, Minister, Rabbi)		
Accountant/CPA		
Estate Liquidator		
Personal Property Appraiser		
Handyman		
Cleaning Service		
Veteran's Administration		
Realtor		
Real Estate Appraiser		
Newspaper(s)		
Neighbors/Friends		

Father's Medical Checklist

Information About You

Name _____

Address _____

Birth Date _____   Blood Type _____

Height _____   Weight _____

Pharmacy _____   Phone _____

Primary Care _____   Phone _____

Other
Physicians _____   Phone _____

Emergency
Contact   Phone _____

_____   _____

_____   _____

Vaccinations (please note the date of the immunization)

Influenza _____   Tetanus/Diphtheria _____

MMR _____   Pneumococcal _____

_____   _____

_____   _____

_____   _____

Medical Conditions

- ❏ Asthma
- ❏ Heart Disease
- ❏ High Blood Pressure
- ❏
- ❏

- ❏ Cancer
- ❏ Kidney Disease
- ❏ Other
- ❏
- ❏

Important Health Care Documents

- ❏ Health Care Proxy
- ❏ Location of Document
- ❏
- ❏

- ❏ Health Care Durable Power of Attorney
- ❏ Interested in Organ or Tissue Donation
- ❏
- ❏

Health Insurance

_____

_____

Mother's Medical Checklist

Information About You

Name	_____
Address	_____

Birth Date	_____	Blood Type	_____
Height	_____	Weight	_____
Pharmacy	_____	Phone	_____
Primary Care	_____	Phone	_____
Other Physicians	_____	Phone	_____
Emergency Contact	_____	Phone	_____

Vaccinations (please note the date of the immunization)

Influenza	_____	Tetanus/Diphtheria	_____
MMR	_____	Pneumococcal	_____
	_____		_____
	_____		_____
	_____		_____

Medical Conditions

❑ Asthma

❑ Heart Disease

❑ High Blood Pressure

❑

❑

❑ Cancer

❑ Kidney Disease

❑ Other

❑

❑

Important Health Care Documents

❑ Health Care Proxy

❑ Location of Document

❑

❑

❑ Health Care Durable Power of Attorney

❑ Interested in Organ or Tissue Donation

❑

❑

Health Insurance

_____

_____

Over-the-Counter / Discontinued Medications

Over-the-Counter Medications		Discontinued Medications/Products (Due to Allergies, Side Effects, or Reactions)		
		Medication/Food/ Environment	Date (mm/yy)	Allergy, Side Effects, Intolerance Experienced
Allergy Relief/ Antihistamines				
Cough/Cold				
Aspirin/Other (for Pain/				
Antacids				
Laxatives				
Sleep Assistance				
Diet Pills				
Herbal/Dietary Supplements				
St. John's Wort				
Gingko Biloba				
Kava Kava				

Other (be sure to list on Medications)

_____

_____

_____

_____

_____

_____

_____

MEDICAL NOTES:

Medication List

Sample Medication	Medication #1
Name of Medication: (brand/generic names)	Name of Medication: (brand/generic names)
Generic abcdef	
Prescribed By: (doctor name and specialty)	Prescribed By: (doctor name and specialty)
Dr. Jones, cardiologist	
Dosage: (mg/units/puffs/drops/tablets)	Dosage: (mg/units/puffs/drops/tablets
10 mg	
When is Medication Taken: (am/pm/bedtime/meals)	When is Medication Taken: (am/pm/bedtime/meals)
1 pill, two times/day with meals	
Purpose: (what does medication do?)	Purpose: (what does medication do?)
Blood pressure	
Possible Side Effects:	Possible Side Effects:
Dizziness, numbness in arms, fainting	
Notes/Changes:	Notes/Changes:
03/15/11 – reviewed by Dr. Jones, lowered dosage	
to 5 mg per day	
Medication #2	**Medication #3**
Name of Medication: (brand/generic names)	Name of Medication: (brand/generic names)
Prescribed By: (doctor name and specialty)	Prescribed By: (doctor name and specialty)
Dosage: (mg/units/puffs/drops/tablets)	Dosage: (mg/units/puffs/drops/tablets)
When is Medication Taken: (am/pm/bedtime/meals)	When is Medication Taken: (am/pm/bedtime/meals)
Purpose: (what does medication do?)	Purpose: (what does medication do?)
Possible Side Effects:	Possible Side Effects:
Notes/Changes:	Notes/Changes:

Medication List

Medication #4	Medication #5
Name of Medication: (brand/generic names)	Name of Medication: (brand/generic names)
Prescribed By: (doctor name and specialty)	Prescribed By: (doctor name and specialty)
Dosage: (mg/units/puffs/drops/tablets)	Dosage: (mg/units/puffs/drops/tablets
When is Medication Taken: (am/pm/bedtime/meals)	When is Medication Taken: (am/pm/bedtime/meals)
Purpose: (what does medication do?)	Purpose: (what does medication do?)
Possible Side Effects:	Possible Side Effects:
Notes/Changes:	Notes/Changes:

Medication #6	Medication #7
Name of Medication: (brand/generic names)	Name of Medication: (brand/generic names)
Prescribed By: (doctor name and specialty)	Prescribed By: (doctor name and specialty)
Dosage: (mg/units/puffs/drops/tablets)	Dosage: (mg/units/puffs/drops/tablets)
When is Medication Taken: (am/pm/bedtime/meals)	When is Medication Taken: (am/pm/bedtime/meals)
Purpose: (what does medication do?)	Purpose: (what does medication do?)
Possible Side Effects:	Possible Side Effects:
Notes/Changes:	Notes/Changes:

Phone Notification Directory

NAME (Who to call for notification)	PHONE NUMBER

Wish List Spreadsheet (Example)
(hypothetical appraised values)

PERSON	ITEM	APPRAISED VALUE	DUPLICATE WISHES?	WITH WHOM?
Karen	Mantel clock	$200	No	
	Silver bell collection	$250	No	
	Painting in Mom's room	$375	No	
	Painting in spare room	$175	No	
	Rooster statue in kitchen	$25	No	
	Mom's perfume bottles	$150	No	
	Antique school desk	$35	No	
	Mom's childhood doll	$75	No	
	Grandma's wedding quilt	$375	No	
	Sterling silver flatware	$1,700	No	
	Centerpiece in dining room	$45	No	
	Gold curio cabinet in living room	$225	No	
	Chandelier, crystal and brass	$1,500	Yes	Jimmy
	Grandfather's tall case clock	$9,000	Yes	Jimmy
	Four-gallon pottery churn	$175	No	
	Mom's diamond earrings	$850	No	
	Antique fireplace screen	$695	Yes	Jimmy
	Dining room table and chairs	$1,000	Yes	Jimmy
	Karen's TOTAL	$16,850		

PERSON	ITEM	APPRAISED VALUE	DUPLICATE WISHES?	WITH WHOM?
Jimmy	Grandfather's pocket watch	$175	No	
	Power tools in garage	$250	No	
	Grandfather's oak roll top desk	$1,200	No	
	Dad's pipe collection on stand	$55	No	
	Dad's letter opener	$15	No	
	Dining room table and chairs	$1,000	Yes	Karen
	La-Z-Boy chair in den	$250	No	
	Bronze eagle statue on Dad's desk	$375	No	
	John Deere garden tractor	$2,100	No	
	Chandelier, crystal and brass	$1,500	Yes	Karen
	Grandfather's tall case clock	$9,000	Yes	Karen
	Antique fireplace screen	$695	Yes	Karen
	Jimmy's TOTAL	$16,615		

Wish List Spreadsheet
(Make as many copies as necessary)

PERSON	ITEM	APPRAISED VALUE	DUPLICATE WISHES?	WITH WHOM?

Wish List Spreadsheet
(Make as many copies as necessary)

PERSON	ITEM	APPRAISED VALUE	DUPLICATE WISHES?	WITH WHOM?

Home Inventory List

ITEM	Manufacturer/Model/ Serial Number	Purchase Price	Date of Purchase	Current Value	Condition	Location	Category
Porcelain Vase, blue floral	Wedgewood	$500	1970	$800	Excellent	Dining Room	China

ITEM	Manufacturer/Model/ Serial Number	Purchase Price	Date of Purchase	Current Value	Condition	Location	Category

ITEM	Manufacturer/Model/ Serial Number	Purchase Price	Date of Purchase	Current Value	Condition	Location	Category

NOTES:

_____

_____

_____

_____

_____

_____

_____

_____

_____

_____

_____

_____

_____

_____

Room by Room Walkthrough

Room	Special Challenges	Solution to Challenge	Timeline	Donation	Sale
Living	grand piano – heavy, old	call piano specialist	by June 1st	No	Maybe
Den	lots of old files, paperwork	organize, call shredder	by July 1st	No	No
Garage	excess of nails, bolts, tools, lumber	call Habitat for Humanity	by April 15th	Yes	No
Master Bedroom	antique oil painting	call appraiser	by May 15th	No	Yes

Living Room					
Dining Room					

Room	Special Challenges	Solution to Challenge	Timeline	Donation	Sale
Dining Room					
Kitchen					
Bedroom 1					

Room	Special Challenges	Solution to Challenge	Timeline	Donation	Sale
Bedroom 1					
Bedroom 2					

Room	Special Challenges	Solution to Challenge	Timeline	Donation	Sale
Bedroom 3					
Bedroom 4					

Room	Special Challenges	Solution to Challenge	Timeline	Donation	Sale
Den/Office					
Garage					

Room	Special Challenges	Solution to Challenge	Timeline	Donation	Sale
Basement/Attic					
Other					

NOTES:

Donation List

ITEM DESCRIPTION	TO WHOM	VALUE	DATE
Sleeper sofa	Habitat for Humanity	$100	02/05/11

NOTES:

NOTES:

NOTES:

CPSIA information can be obtained at www.ICGtesting.com
Printed in the USA
BVOW06s1249071114

373754BV00002B/39/P